St. Louis

impressions

FARCOUNTRY
PRESS

photography by Scott R. Avetta

text by Tom Uhlenbrock

Dedicated to my mother, Audrey, and in memory of my father, Richard. I am so grateful for all that you have done. My vision is a result of your wisdom.

TITLE PAGE: Twilight illuminates the windows of downtown buildings as the span of the Gateway Arch peers between the Municipal Courts building and the tower of Union Station. The domed Old Courthouse—site of the Dred Scott case, in which slaves Dred and Harriet Scott sued for their freedom—stands below the arch.

RIGHT: Sunrise colors the Mississippi River a rosy red on the St. Louis riverfront.

FRONT COVER: Lightning crackles over the St. Louis skyline, which is dominated by the Gateway Arch, symbol of the westward migration by early pioneers.

BACK COVER: Fields of tulips decorate the grounds of the Jewel Box in Forest Park each spring.

ISBN 10: 1-56037-399-7
ISBN 13: 978-1-56037-399-5
Photography © 2006 by Scott R. Avetta
© 2006 Farcountry Press
Text by Tom Uhlenbrock

For more information about our books write Farcountry Press, P.O. Box 5630, Helena, MT 59604; call (800) 821-3874; or visit www.farcountrypress.com.

Created, produced, and designed in the United States.
Printed in China.

10 09 08 07 06   1 2 3 4 5

Foreword

by **Tom Uhlenbrock,**
Travel Writer,
St. Louis Post-Dispatch

ABOVE: A statue of poet and historian Friedrich von Schiller stands in St. Louis Park on 21st Street. Von Schiller was an eighteenth-century German poet and historian who was a favorite among immigrants who came to the city.

RIGHT: Winter adds an icy chill to the lake at Pagoda Circle in front of the Muny Opera in Forest Park.

Where the nation's two great rivers meet, that is St. Louis. The confluence of the Mississippi and Missouri rivers long has been a gathering place. Ancient peoples were building fortress-like temples at Cahokia Mounds—on the Illinois side of the metropolitan area—about the same time the Egyptians were constructing pyramids along the Nile.

The ancient ones were long gone, leaving behind only their earthen mounds and pottery shards, when French fur traders Pierre Laclede and René Auguste Chouteau arrived from New Orleans in 1763. They selected a site below the swampy confluence for their new fur-trading town and named it St. Louis in honor of Louis IX, the king of France.

Laclede predicted that St. Louis would become one of the finest cities on the continent "by its locality and central position."

When Meriwether Lewis and William Clark arrived in 1804 to prepare for their monumental trek west, St. Louis was a bustling port of hunters, voyageurs, fur trappers, and rivermen—and an elite class of traders who capitalized on their efforts. After the Corps of Discovery's successful expedition, Clark made his home in St. Louis; his grave can be found amid the imposing monuments of Bellefontaine Cemetery on the city's north side.

Some 100 years later, St. Louis was the fourth-largest city in the United States and the center of the world's attention when it hosted the 1904 World's Fair, also know as the Louisiana Purchase Exposition. As Judy Garland sang, the world turned out to "meet me at the fair…."

The World's Fair played host to 20 million visitors, who witnessed the public debut of air conditioning and spoke by wireless telegraph to cities 1,500 miles away. They saw re-creations of jungles in the Philippines, Japanese gardens, and the holy sites of Jerusalem. The 1904 Olympics, the first held in the United States, also took place at the St. Louis World's Fair.

The fair was held in Forest Park, which was established in 1876 and, at the time, was a 40-minute carriage ride from the city. Today, the 1,293-acre green space is located at the heart of St. Louis and celebrated its 130th birthday with a $100-million makeover.

Forest Park is the home of the Art Museum, History Museum, Zoo, Muny Opera, Science Center, Planetarium, Steinberg Skating Rink, and the Jewel Box, an art deco-building that features seasonal floral displays.

The park was the city's most beloved and visited attraction until October 28, 1965, when construction of a giant, stainless-steel arch in a park overlooking the Mississippi was completed. The Gateway

swaying can be uneasy on the stomach.

The photogenic arch is a treat from any angle, although the best view may be from a prone position on the grass beneath, with clouds drifting over the shimmering legs.

Although St. Louis may have been bypassed in its national status by faster-growing cities with much less history, it still has a claim to some world-class residents:

• The St. Louis Zoo is constantly updating its facilities to retain its ranking among the country's finest—and it's free.

• The Missouri Botanical Garden is among the nation's oldest, with Japanese and Chinese gardens and the Climatron, a geodesic dome teeming with tropical plants.

• The Anheuser-Busch brewery, the world's largest, has its historic headquarters open for tours, as does Grant's Farm, the 281-acre ancestral home of the Busch family. The farm is the home of more than 1,000 animals, including the famous Clydesdales.

Arch, officially called the Jefferson National Expansion Memorial, symbolizes the spirit of the pioneers who passed through the city on their way west.

Their story, and that of Lewis and Clark, is detailed in the Museum of Westward Expansion, which lies beneath the span. The museum's exhibits include presidential peace medals, mounted animal specimens, and an authentic Indian tepee with artifacts.

Visitors can ride tram cars up the arch's "legs" 630 feet to the top and peer out windows for a bird's-eye view of the city. But beware, the arch was designed to give up to 18 inches in strong winds, and the

• The St. Louis Cardinals are a perennial National League power, with a legacy of All Stars that includes Stan Musial, Bob Gibson, and Ozzie Smith.

• The Cardinals and the NFL's Rams both have new homes near the Mississippi River, and the architectural gems of the downtown mercantile center are being renovated into lofts for another generation of city dwellers.

St. Louis, the gathering place by the rivers, begins anew.

LEFT: Rain on a windowpane creates a Monet-like view of flowers blooming at the Missouri Botanical Garden. Founded by Henry Shaw in 1859, it is one of the oldest botanical institutes in the country and a National Historic Landmark.

BELOW: The Jefferson Barracks National Cemetery is the final resting place for many of America's soldiers. The cemetery was established in 1866 on a bluff overlooking the Mississippi River south of the city.

RIGHT: Children beat the heat at Mighty Mud Mania in Jefferson Barracks Park. The annual event for children ages five to fifteen features an obstacle course through a pit of slippery, gooey mud.

BELOW: An American kestrel is one of the many species of raptors found at the World Bird Sanctuary, a rehabilitation center in suburban St. Louis.

ABOVE: The clock tower of the restored Union Station stands like a sentinel over the Carl Milles fountain *The Meeting of the Waters.*

RIGHT: Carl Milles's fountain symbolizes the confluence of the Mississippi and Missouri rivers north of the city.

BBQ RIBS
$12.99
Pork
WE HAVE
HAM HOCKS
SMOKED JOWL
CRAWFISH
WHOLE
TAIL MEAT
ALLIGATOR
MEAT
SAUSAGE
BOUDIN
CRACKLIN'S
SAUSAGE
$6.99
1 LB PKG.

ABOVE: Penguins are among the favorite attractions at the world-renowned St. Louis Zoo.

LEFT: You can buy almost anything at Soulard Farmers Market, including alligator sausage. Established in 1779, Soulard is the oldest farmers' market west of the Mississippi.

ABOVE: Chain of Rocks Bridge, which once carried historic Route 66 over the Mississippi River, has reopened as a recreational bridge for pedestrians and cyclists.

RIGHT: Laumeier Sculpture Park features 96 acres of outdoor sculptures, including Alexander Liberman's *The Way*.

ABOVE: The venerable Chase Hotel towers above Forest Park. The Chase, which recently underwent a $100-million facelift, has been a favorite spot for travelers since the 1920s. Many of its rooms overlook the park, which is the home of the St. Louis Zoo, Art Museum, and History Museum.

RIGHT: A statue of King Louis IX of France, the city's namesake, stands outside the St. Louis Art Museum.

ABOVE: Carriages take riders over the cobblestone streets of the Laclede's Landing entertainment district.

RIGHT: Buildings in the historic Old Town of Florissant date back to the 1790s.

ABOVE: A giant Vess soda bottle is the symbol of the emerging Bottle District north of downtown.

LEFT: The Soulard area is one of the oldest in the city, with homes dating from the mid- to late 1800s. Now a mix of old and new, the neighborhood boasts cafes and clubs that offer live music.

ABOVE: The *Tom Sawyer II* excursion boat carries passengers below the historic Eads Bridge on the St. Louis riverfront.

RIGHT: St. Louis is home of Anheuser-Busch, the world's largest brewery, and its trademark Clydesdale horses.

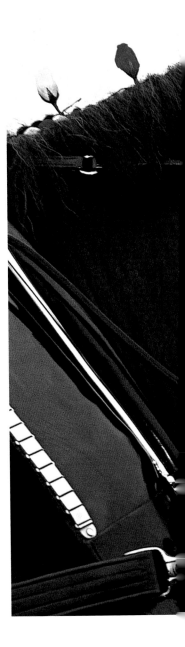

LEFT: A half-moon rides the evening sky, just below a leg of the 630-foot Gateway Arch.

BELOW: The arch's reflection in an Old Courthouse window.

FACING PAGE, NEAR: The grounds of the arch are the location of the city's annual Fourth of July celebration.

FACING PAGE, TOP: The new Busch Stadium has views of the city skyline and arch.

FACING PAGE, BOTTOM: The dome of the Old Courthouse sits beneath the arch near Kiener Plaza, which is decorated for Christmas.

LEFT: A sprawling, concrete serpent guards the entrance to City Museum. Housed in the 600,000-square-foot former International Shoe Co., the museum is an eclectic mix of children's playground, funhouse, and surrealistic pavilion, all created out of found and recycled objects by sculptor Bob Cassilly.

BELOW, LEFT AND RIGHT: Stone sculptures decorate the Soldier's Memorial. The memorial was opened in 1938 to honor St. Louisans who died in World War I.

ABOVE: The arching stem of a tulip creates an abstract delight in a flowerbed at the Missouri Botanical Garden.

LEFT: The stunning art-deco Jewel Box showcases permanent and seasonal floral displays.

LEFT: Graffiti artists were invited to decorate the floodwall near the McArthur Bridge, which opened to the public in 1917 and spans the Mississippi River.

BELOW: Forsythia blooms are the first sign of spring in the Soulard area.

ABOVE: Prairie dogs are among the residents of the St. Louis Zoo, which is free to all visitors.

RIGHT: A goal of the St. Louis Zoo is to give visitors up-close and personal visits with its animals.

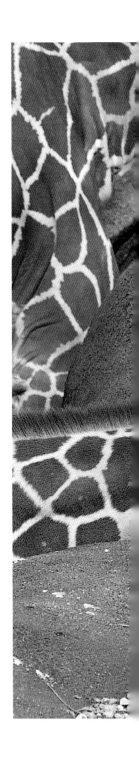

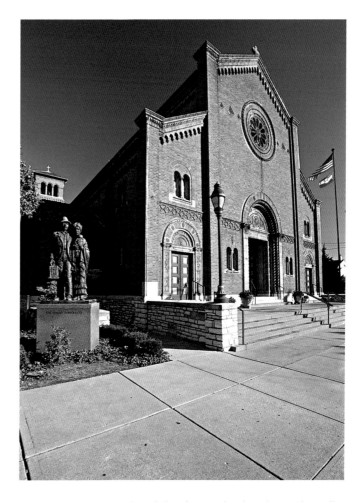

ABOVE: St. Ambrose Church has been a landmark on The Hill since 1926. Named for its proximity to the city's highest point, The Hill is an Italian-American community known for its bakeries and restaurants. A statue next to the church honors Italian immigrants.

LEFT: The Flight Cage at the St. Louis Zoo dates back to the 1904 World's Fair. It now houses several indigenous species of birds.

ABOVE: An old hitching post still stands in Lafayette Square. The area was among the city's earliest districts and catered to the carriage trade.

RIGHT: First set aside as a park just before the Civil War, Lafayette Square was developed into a Victorian-era showplace, with gardens, gazebos, a bandstand, and a boathouse.

ABOVE: A northern mockingbird finds a winter treat.

LEFT: St. Louis is home to several nationally recognized educational institutions, including Washington University.

ABOVE: The renowned artist Ernest Trova is from St. Louis, where many of his trademark *Walking Man* sculptures are displayed. This one depicts six figures atop a tiered black granite base radiating from a central cube.

RIGHT: A giant shoe sculpture marks the headquarters of Brown Shoe Co. Founded in 1878 by George Warren Brown, the company is now a billion-dollar corporation.

LEFT: Traffic streams by the pedestrian bridge that joins the St. Louis Science Center to Forest Park. The center has three floors of interactive exhibits and an Omnimax theater.

BELOW: This work of neon art marks the home of Federhofer's Bakery, which opened in 1957 on Gravois Road on the city's south side.

RIGHT: The lights of downtown buildings add a twinkle to the evening sky.

BELOW: The Morgan Street Brewery won't challenge Anheuser-Busch in volume but it pumps its fair share of microbrews. Founded in 1995, the brewery is in the popular Laclede's Landing entertainment district on the riverfront.

ABOVE: Pasta and Roman Catholics are mainstays of The Hill, the Italian section of the city.

LEFT: Tower Grove Park is a special place for joggers, cyclists, and newlyweds. The park was a gift to St. Louis residents from botanist Henry Shaw in 1868.

LEFT: Ted Drewes Frozen Custard stand has been drawing summertime crowds since 1929.

BELOW: A fire hydrant on The Hill bears the national colors of Italy.

The interior of the New Cathedral of St. Louis boasts the largest mosaic collection in the world (*left*). The Cathedral features a Romanesque exterior with a Byzantine-style interior (*far left*).

ABOVE: Crown Candy Kitchen in north St. Louis has been tempting folks with its ice cream and other sweet confections since 1913.

LEFT: The annual Balloon Glow in Forest Park precedes a "hare and hound" balloon race over the metropolitan area.

St. Louis celebrates its French heritage with a Mardi Gras celebration that rivals the one held farther south on the Mississippi *(right)*. The dog parade is a popular Mardi Gras event *(above)*.

ABOVE: The paper kite butterfly is one of dozens of species found in the Sophia M. Sachs Butterfly House in Faust Park.

LEFT: The glass conservatory of the Sachs Butterfly House is the home of hundreds of butterflies in free flight. The landscaped grounds offer the opportunity to see native butterflies in a natural environment.

57

LEFT: Blueberry Hill is the anchor of the Delmar Loop entertainment area. The bar/restaurant presents live music in the Duck Room, which is named for the duck walk done onstage by St. Louis–native Chuck Berry.

BELOW: The restored Pageant Theatre in the Loop is one of the city's hottest live music venues.

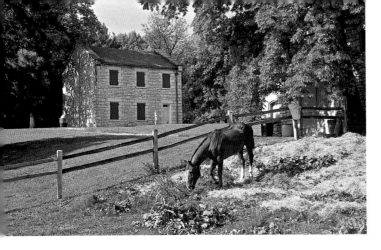

ABOVE: A historic stable and house built in the late 1800s are among the attractions at Jefferson Barracks Park.

RIGHT: Grant's Cabin was built by Ulysses S. Grant in 1848 as part of a farm he called Hardscrabble.

BELOW: Clydesdales roam the pastures at Grant's Farm, a 281-acre nature preserve that was the ancestral home of the Anheuser-Busch brewing family. The farm is still owned and operated by the brewery and is open to the public for tours.

ABOVE: The historic Eads Bridge stretches over the Mississippi River to the Illinois side of the metropolitan area and the Casino Queen gambling complex.

FACING PAGE: The McDonnell Planetarium in Forest Park shows its many colors.

ABOVE: The Old Courthouse overlooking the riverfront is the scene of the city's annual Fourth of July celebration.

RIGHT: Autumn leaves shower a Chinese pavilion in Tower Grove Park.

ABOVE: The giant fruit of the osage orange tree is a favorite with the area's squirrels.

RIGHT: Birders from throughout the country flock to St. Louis to see Eurasian tree sparrows, a species that was released by immigrants in 1870. The St. Louis area is the only place in North America where the birds are known to live.

FAR RIGHT: A sprinkler splashing against a picket fence makes a refreshing scene in Soulard.

ABOVE: Built in 1882 by Henry Shaw, the Linnean House at the Missouri Botanical Garden is the oldest continually operated greenhouse west of the Mississippi River. It was named after botanist Carl Linnaeus.

LEFT: Giant water lilies cover the pond in front of the Climatron geodesic dome at the Missouri Botanical Garden. Inside the dome is a jungle of tropical plants from around the world.

ABOVE: The St. Louis Cardinals, perennial powers in the National League, started the 2007 season in a new version of Busch Stadium.

RIGHT: The Cardinals consistently draw more than three million fans a year, one of the top attendance marks in baseball.

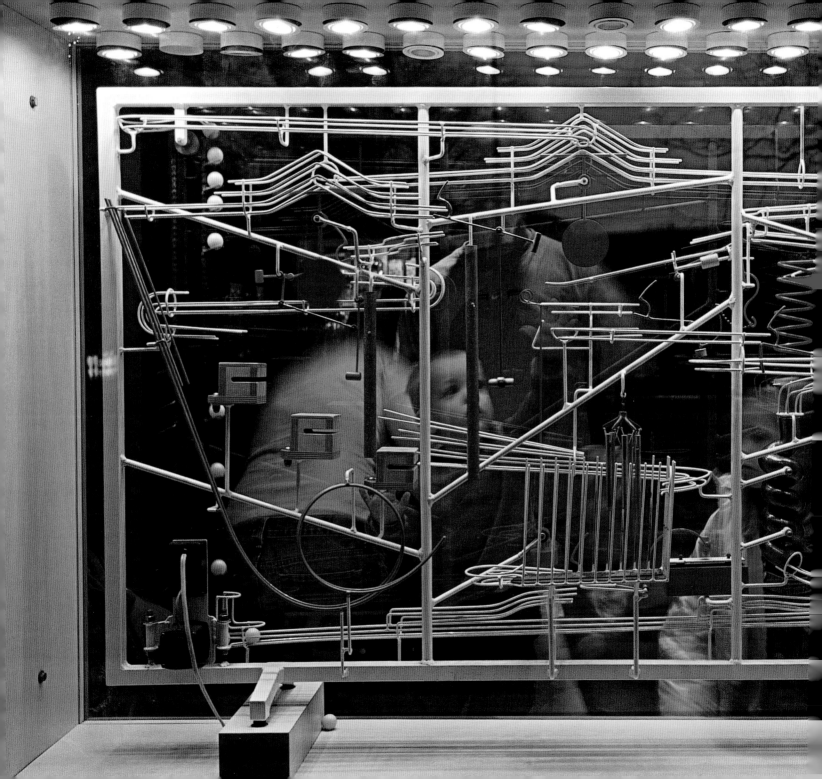

ABOVE: The cathedral at St. Louis University is among the architectural gems on the impressive midtown campus. The university was founded in 1818.

LEFT: The Magic House has been voted one of the nation's top attractions for kids. The house has numerous interactive exhibits at a restored mansion in the suburb of Kirkwood.

ABOVE: The maze at the Missouri Botanical Garden is a favorite with younger visitors.

FACING PAGE: The Japanese Garden is a rainbow of colors in spring.

ABOVE: Rams running back Steven Jackson celebrates a touchdown at the team's home, the Edward Jones Dome.
PHOTO BY CHRIS LEE OF THE *ST. LOUIS POST-DISPATCH.*

RIGHT: Rams wide receiver Torry Holt hauls in a 40-yard touchdown pass against San Francisco.
PHOTO BY CHRIS LEE OF THE *ST. LOUIS POST-DISPATCH.*

ABOVE: The Fox Theatre opened in 1929 and received a restoration that made it one of the country's grand old surviving theaters.

LEFT: Fountains and a fiery sunset add drama to the Grand Basin below the St. Louis Art Museum in Forest Park. The park was established in 1876 and recently received a $100-million makeover.

PHOTO BY RUTH HOYT

Scott R. Avetta

Scott R. Avetta is a native of St. Louis, Missouri, with an undergraduate degree in business management from Maryville University. His work has been published in many books, including *Illinois Impressions, Missouri Simply Beautiful, The Ozarks, St. Louis Seen and Unseen, St. Louis—For the Record, Last Stand of the Tallgrass Prairie, Lewis and Clark's Journey Across Missouri,* and *America's National Parks.*

Scott's images are on permanent display in Alton, Illinois, at the National Great Rivers Museum. Additional works have been published in *Landscape Architecture* and *Missouri Life Magazine.* The National Audubon Society and other organizations have used his photographs for advertising, calendars, postcards, websites, and newsletters.

Scott teaches photography at the Missouri Botanical Garden. He has been involved in photographic instruction with Kodak-sponsored workshops, the Missouri Department of Conservation, and Public Lands Day. Scott is president, board of directors member, and program chairman of Missouri Nature and Environmental Photographers (MoNEP). Nature-oriented organizations such as the Earth Day Celebration, the Open Door Animal Sanctuary, and the World Bird Sanctuary have captured his interest.